Estate Planning in Florida

A Concise and Complete Guide to

Peace of Mind

by
Dean Hanewinckel
Attorney At Law

Law Offices of Dean Hanewinckel, P.A.
2650 South McCall Road
Englewood, Florida 34224
(941) 473-2828

ISBN: 978-0-9818233-2-4

This publication is designed to provide accurate and authoritative information with regard to the subject matter covered. Despite the fact that the author is an attorney, neither he nor the publisher is engaged in rendering legal advice or other professional services in this publication. This publication is not intended to create an attorney-client relationship between the author and any reader. If legal advice or other expert assistance is required, the services of a competent professional should be sought.

TABLE OF CONTENTS

The Importance of Estate Planning

The topic of Estate Planning is not the most popular subject. Not many people enjoy contemplating their mortality. It is however a necessary process for those who wish to ease the burden on their loved ones after they are gone. Estate Planning can also be thought of as an opportunity to accomplish great things. It can be a means for you to leave a lasting legacy to your family and to your community. This book will explain strategies and give you examples of how you can combine charitable giving with your estate plan to accomplish some amazing results.

As an Estate Planning and probate attorney, I have seen probate cases that range from tedious to unmitigated disasters. The cost, paperwork and incessant delays of the probate process tend to bring out the very worst in some families.

In my experience I have found that the success of a person's estate administration is strongly dependent upon the quality of that person's estate plan. Simply stated, those who make the effort to properly plan, make it much easier on those they leave behind.

In fact, the most motivated estate planning clients are those who have been through the battle of administering a parent's poorly planned estate. They vow that they will never put their spouse and children through the grueling and frustrating experience they just experienced.

What constitutes a good estate plan? It depends upon the person and his or her circumstances. Usually, it involves creating a scenario to pass your estate to the beneficiaries of your choice in the most efficient manner possible.

This means eliminating or reducing taxes and expenses. The lack of an estate plan usually means your heirs will incur the hefty costs of the court supervised probate process. This book will give you all the gruesome details of probate and then tell you how to avoid it.

It also means addressing Florida law that may circumvent your wishes and result in unintended and even unwanted consequences. If you are in a second marriage, have a minor child or want to pass on your homestead property, you must comply with or exempt the transaction from the laws of Florida. We will explore the strange and complicated laws that are unique to Florida and how to stay out of those traps.

It means selecting and ensuring that the proper person will administer your estate. The lack of documentation, such as a Will or trust that designates a specific administrator often results in vicious fights among family members or the appointment of someone who is not competent to handle the work.

It means matching the assets of your estate with the proper beneficiaries. I know of a situation where a brother and sister did not speak to each other for over 20 years because of a dispute over the distribution of a chair from their mother's estate!

And it means protecting your privacy and that of your family. The probate process is a court proceeding open to the public. That strange lady across the street who is always peeking through her blinds can go to the clerk's office, pull your file and find out what you owned, what debts you had and who you left your estate to. Later in this book, we will discuss how poor estate planning led to the invasion of the privacy of James Gandolfini's family.

An effective estate plan is not a fill-in-the-blanks, one-size-fits-all solution. There are many tools you can employ to reach your estate planning goals. However, not every tool is appropriate for your circumstance. Each person's goals, assets, debts and family dynamics are different. What may make a great estate plan for one person, may lead to disastrous results for another.

This book will introduce you to the various estate planning tools, describe the pros and cons of each and explain how they may or may not fit in to your estate plan.

I'm sure you've noticed that this book is not very long. My intent in writing it was to give you a concise introduction to common methods of estate planning. I didn't want to bog you down in boring legalese or the tedious estate tax regulations. If you wish to delve deeper into a subject, I invite you to visit my estate planning website:

www.EstatePlanningInFlorida.com

You can also call my office at (941) 473-2828 and I will be happy to discuss how a certain estate planning tool or strategy may fit your circumstances.

Law Offices of Dean Hanewinckel, P.A.
2650 South McCall Road
Englewood, Florida 34224

What Is Probate and Should You Avoid It?

One of the most misunderstood concepts of law to the layman is the probate process. Many persons are named as personal representatives in their parent's, other family member's or friend's Wills without knowing what the job entails. As a result the probate process is often feared and some will go to great lengths to avoid it. This chapter will attempt to explain what probate is and why it is necessary for so many people.

Simply defined, probate is the procedure necessary to establish the validity of a Will. The process of collecting a decedent's assets, paying his bills and taxes, and distributing what is left to his heirs or beneficiaries is actually called "administration" of the estate although it has become common to refer to this entire process as probate. There are two types of probate administration under Florida law: formal administration and summary administration.

Summary administration is an abbreviated proceeding for smaller estates. Summary administration is available if the gross value of the probate estate is not greater than $75,000 or the decedent has been dead for at least two years.

Estates can be either testate, where the decedent has left a valid Will, or intestate, where there is no Will. In an administration of an intestate estate the laws of the state of Florida will determine how the assets are distributed (We'll talk about that in the next Chapter). In a testate estate, the Will acts as a set of instructions to the court, naming a personal representative and directing the disposition of the assets.

Estates subject to probate administration consist of assets owned solely by the decedent with no provision for automatic succession of ownership at death. Examples of automatic succession include beneficiary designations on life insurance policies and annuity contracts, bank accounts held "in trust for" a beneficiary and property owned as joint tenants with a right of survivorship. These assets would not be included in a probate estate and will generally go automatically to the named beneficiary or surviving joint tenant.

Formal administration is started by filing a petition for administration which identifies the decedent, states the approximate nature and value of the estate assets, names the beneficiaries, requests appointment of a personal representative, and, in a testate estate, identifies the Will and requests that it be admitted to probate. All interested persons (as defined by Florida law) must then be served with formal notice of the petition.

If the court finds the petition to be in order and there are no objections to the petition, then the will is admitted to probate, the personal representative is appointed and issued letters of administration. The letters of administration give the personal representative authority granted by the court to act on behalf of the estate.

The personal representative then publishes a notice of administration once a week for 2 consecutive weeks in a newspaper of general circulation in the county where the estate is administered. The notice of administration is intended to notify creditors of the decedent of the administration of the estate so that they may file claims to have any outstanding debts of the decedent paid. The personal representative is also required to serve a copy of the notice on those creditors of which he is aware. As a general rule, the creditors must file a claim with the court within 3 months of the date of the first publication or they will lose all rights to collect their debt.

The personal representative then goes through the process of identifying and collecting the estate assets, objecting to or paying claims, filing tax returns, distributing assets to the proper beneficiaries, paying administration expenses, reporting all of these activities to the court and closing the probate administration. Depending upon the complexity of the estate, this process can take from a few months to a few years to complete.

The personal representative, attorney for the estate and other professionals involved in the administration are entitled by law to compensation. Florida law states that the personal representative may receive a commission payable from the estate assets based upon the value of the estate. For estates less than one million dollars the commission would be three percent of the estate's value. Attorneys for the Personal Representative would also receive a fee (generally 3% of the value of the estate's value).

As you can see, we've identified three reasons to avoid the probate process:

1. **It's time consuming.** A typical formal administration proceeding in Florida takes 8 months to a year to complete.

2. **It's public.** The probate administration is a court proceeding. Many of the documents and information about the decedent and his or her estate are a matter of public record. That creepy old lady who is always looking through her blinds at your house can go down to the courthouse and look through your probate file. She may be able to find out what you owned at death, who you owed money to and who will receive an inheritance from you.

3. **It's expensive.** Probate usually costs from 4% to 8% of the value of your estate. If you owned a house worth $200,000 and stocks and bonds worth another $200,000, the costs of probate would range from $16,000 to $32,000 ! That's money that goes to attorneys, court costs, accountants, etc. Most importantly, that's money that is not going to your loved ones.

Intestate Succession: Dying Without A Will

In Florida, if you die without a Will, the state doesn't take everything – but it does dictate who does. You've probably heard the warning, if you don't draw up a Will, the state will draw one up for you. That is exactly what happens in Florida.

If you die without a Will, your probate estate is considered to be "intestate." In those cases, the distribution of your assets will be governed by Florida's law of intestate succession. It is a directive of what the Florida legislature believes is a fair allocation of your estate. Unfortunately, what the state believes is fair and what you believe is appropriate are often two completely different things. It is important to note that intestate succession only affects property in the probate estate. All jointly owned property with a right of survivorship, all accounts with "Transfer on Death" provisions and all pensions, annuities and insurance policies with properly designated beneficiaries are not affected by intestate succession, because they are not a part of the probate estate. They automatically pass to the surviving joint owners and the beneficiaries named by the decedent. Likewise, property titled in the name of a revocable trust is not part of the probate estate and will pass to the beneficiaries named in the trust.

Any property owned solely by the decedent at the time of his or her death with no contractual means to distribute it will in the probate estate and subject to intestate succession if there is no valid Will.

Leaving A Surviving Spouse. So who gets the property in that situation? That depends on a number of factors. First, did the decedent leave a surviving spouse? If so, the following rules apply:

1. If there is a surviving spouse and the decedent has no living children or grandchildren or great-grandchildren (lineal descendants), then the surviving spouse gets the entire probate estate.

2. If the decedent has lineal descendants, and all of them are also lineal descendants of the surviving spouse, then the surviving spouse gets the first $60,000 of the probate estate and half of the balance of the probate estate. The lineal descendants split the remaining half.

3. If the decedent has lineal descendants, and one or more of them are not lineal descendants of the surviving spouse, then the surviving spouse gets one-half of the probate estate and the lineal descendants divide the other half equally among themselves.

Except For Homestead. If the decedent is survived by a spouse and lineal descendants, then the surviving spouse will receive a life estate in the homestead, and after his or her death, the title to the homestead will pass automatically to the lineal descendants of the decedent who were alive at the time of the decedent's death (not the spouse's death). This distribution to the lineal descendants is made "per stirpes." This means that if one of the decedent's children dies before the decedent, the deceased child's share will be divided equally among the deceased child's children.

No Surviving Spouse. If there is no surviving spouse, then the entire probate estate is distributed as follows:

1. Equally among the lineal descendants of the decedent. This distribution is made "per stirpes,"

2. If there are no lineal descendants (this means no children, grandchildren, great-grandchildren, etc.), then the entire probate estate is distributed to the decedent's father and mother, or to the survivor of them.

3. If the decedent has no lineal descendants and no surviving parents, then the probate estate will divided equally among the decedent's brothers and sisters and their descendants, per stirpes.

4. If we still haven't found anyone to give the estate to, then one-half of the estate will be distributed to the decedent's paternal side of the family and one-half to the decedent's maternal side of the family. In doing this, we will look to the grandparents. If they are not surviving, then to uncles and aunts and their descendants.

5. If there are no relatives of the decedent, then the estate will be divided among the descendants (or other kin as described above) of the last deceased spouse of the decedent.

6. If we still can't find anybody, then to the descendants of the decedent's great-grandparents – but only if any of them were Holocaust victims (seriously).

7. Finally, if there are no persons to receive the estate after going through all of the steps above, then the property will escheat to the State of Florida.

As you can see, dying without a coordinated estate plan can cause unintended consequences and a lot of confusion.

The Last Will and Testament

The Last Will and Testament, commonly called a Will, is the basic estate planning document.

If you have recently moved to Florida, it is always a good idea to have your Will and other estate planning documents reviewed by a Florida attorney. As you will see later in this Chapter, your Will should state that you are a Florida resident and your estate plan should comply with Florida law. If you don't already have an estate plan, now is the time to consider one. You saw in the last chapters how expensive and time consuming probate in Florida can be. Despite this, studies have shown that a vast majority of people in the United States don't have any form of formal estate planning. Not even a Will.

Estate planning is simply the process of structuring your estate in a way to direct how your assets get to the persons you want to receive them in the most efficient manner. It can be as elaborate as setting up a myriad of trusts and foundations or as uncomplicated as writing a simple Will or even doing nothing at all. In Florida, there is a bumper sticker that is popular with many retirees. It says: "I'm Spending My Children's Inheritance." Unfortunately, in many cases, that is the full extent of their estate planning. It has been estimated that a vast majority of our country's population has done no estate planning; not even a simple Will. In those cases, their estate planning will be done by the laws of the state in which they reside. The previous chapter shows how convoluted this can become in Florida. In some cases things will turn out the way that they would have wanted. However, in many cases it will not.

Is My Massachusetts Will Valid in Florida? A problem that can arise is when persons have their Wills and other estate planning documents prepared "up north" and move to Florida. In many cases they rely on the documents as they were drawn up originally without having a Florida attorney review them. Every state has its own distinct and different laws regarding probate and other estate planning matters. Florida law says that courts in Florida will recognize a Will as valid if it is valid in the state where it was drawn up at the time it was drawn up. Keeping that in mind, the first issue is then:

1. Is your Will valid in your previous state? In most cases the Will is presumed valid. However, this issue may open up a challenge in a Will contest case. In such a situation, your heirs may have to prove the Will's validity using an expert legal witness from your previous state. This can be a huge expense to your estate.

2. Is your Will self-proved? Even if the Will is deemed to be valid, Florida law requires it to be "proved" in order to be admitted to probate. This means that a person who has signed the Will as a witness must also sign an oath certifying that you executed the Will with the proper legal formalities and that your were competent at the time.

Florida also provides that a Will may be self-proved. This happens when the testator (testatrix, if female) and the witnesses acknowledge the Will and execute a self-proving affidavit in the presence of a notary. Any Will that is self-proved may be admitted to probate without testimony of the attending witnesses. Many states do not customarily self-prove Wills. In these cases the witnesses must be found and they must sign an oath before a judge, clerk or deputy clerk, or court-appointed commissioner, that the Will being offered for probate is the same Will he witnessed the decedent sign. Imagine trying to track down the person who witnessed your Will 40 years ago in Illinois.

Also, even if the witness can be found, he can't sign the oath in front of any notary. He either must sign in the presence of a deputy clerk of a Florida court or a notary commissioned by the Florida probate judge to acknowledge the oath. This procedure adds time and expense to the probate proceeding and should be avoided when possible by drawing up a new Florida Will.

3. Does the person named to serve as your personal representative qualify under Florida law? Florida law requires the personal representative of your estate to either be a) a Florida resident, or b) related to you. Many people name friends form their old state in their Will to be the personal representative (or executor). If these friends are not Florida residents at the time of the administration of your estate, they will not qualify and the court may appoint someone you do not want.

4. Homestead. Florida has very strict and unusual laws regarding the distribution of homestead after a person's death. I will discuss this in a later chapter. If you are married, you can only leave the homestead to your spouse. If you try to do otherwise, the law overrules your wishes and creates a life estate in the surviving spouse and, after he or she dies, leaves your share of the homestead to your lineal descendants – whether that is what you wanted or not.

This can wreak havoc on the estate plans of couples in second marriages who only want to leave their estate to their children. This can also cause problems with couples who have set up A-B Trusts to minimize or avoid estate taxes. The formula for distribution of such a trust may cause the homestead to be distributed to the B Trust, which would violate the homestead law and result in the situation described above.

5. Does your Durable Power of Attorney comply with Florida's new law? Florida recently revamped its durable power of attorney law. Many powers given to the attorney-in-fact (or agent) must be specifically authorized by the principal, or they may not be honored. This has the potential of leading to unwanted guardianship proceedings if you become incapacitated. Update your durable power of attorney to comply with current Florida law.

6. Does your old state recognize you as a resident of Florida? If you look at your current

Will, it will likely say (usually in the first paragraph) that you are a resident of your prior state. Some states take that declaration very seriously. They reason that a Florida resident wouldn't have a Will that states he is a resident of Pennsylvania.

This was the ruling in a 1992 case in the Pennsylvania Commonwealth Court. The court ruled that a person who died in Florida was a Pennsylvania resident and subject to Pennsylvania tax, despite the fact that he received a Florida homestead exemption, had a Florida vehicle registration and driver's license, had bank accounts in Florida, filed his federal income taxes with a Florida address and spent eight months of each year in Florida. The court stated that its decision was based largely on the declaration in his Will that he was a Pennsylvania resident.

As you can see, failing to have your estate plan comply with Florida law can have some serious consequences. If you have made the decision to become a Florida resident, having a Florida attorney review your estate planning documents is as important as changing your drivers license and applying for homestead.

For these reasons, and because you want your Will to state that you are a resident of Florida, you should have your out-of-state Will reviewed by a

Florida attorney, and in most cases, you should have a new Florida Will prepared.

What exactly is a Will, and Doesn't It Avoid Probate? A Will is a document that gives instructions to the Personal Representative and the probate court as to how your assets will pass to your heirs and beneficiaries after your death. Any assets that pass to your heirs through a Will are *guaranteed to go through probate*.

Your Will should have four main parts. The first is the nomination of a "Personal Representative" (sometimes called an executor in other states) who will manage and administer your estate after your death. You may also appoint someone to serve as guardian for your minor children.

The second is the statement directing how your assets will be distributed to your beneficiaries.

The third part of the Will specifies any special powers or authority that the Personal Representative will have to administer the estate. These powers include the power to sell real estate without court approval.

Finally, there is the execution portion of the Will. This is where the testator (man who makes the will) or the testatrix (woman who makes the will) signs the document as his or her Last Will and Testament and where the attesting witnesses also sign the Will. It may also contain a self-proving affidavit as described earlier.

Advantages of a Will. A Will provides a plan for distributing your assets at the time of your death and allows you to decide who will be the Personal Representative of your estate. The Will is a pro-active method of planning your estate and gives you a large degree of control as to what happens to your assets after you are gone.

Disadvantages of a Will. A Will does not avoid probate. Any assets passing through the Will are subject to the costs, delays and lack of privacy of the probate process. Generally, probate administration costs between 4% and 8% of the total gross value of the portion of your estate passing through probate. These costs include Personal Representative fees, attorney's fees, court costs and publication fees. Probate administration also takes a minimum of five months to complete and it is not unusual for a typical estate to drag on for a year or longer. Finally, probate proceedings are a matter of public record. Anyone can find out who your estate is distributed to and, even though the inventory of your estate is not open to the public, there are methods for finding out what assets are in your estate and the value.

Also, a Will only becomes valid at your death. It does not address incapacity during your lifetime. An estate plan that only consists of a Will does not prevent the necessity of a guardianship if you are unable to manage your affairs during your lifetime.

Simple Methods of Avoiding Probate

If you wish to avoid probate, your estate planning must consist of something more than a Will. The following is a list of tools you can use to leave certain assets to your heirs without probate.

Transfer on Death. Transfer on Death (also commonly referred to as "TOD") is a form of securities registration that allows you to name one or more beneficiaries to whom your securities account would pass at your death. The brokerage firm or other entity that accepts the Transfer on Death registration agrees to deliver the securities according to your direction. Any assets passing to a beneficiary as a result of a TOD registration are outside of the probate estate and thus avoid probate.

Advantages of Transfer on Death. TOD registration allows you to maintain complete control of assets during your life and provide for the distribution, outside of probate, to the persons of your choice after your death. The beneficiaries have no ownership interest in the securities during your lifetime. In fact, you can change the TOD designation at any time prior to your death.

Disadvantages of Transfer on Death. TOD only covers assets registered or held in the TOD account. Assets owned outside of TOD accounts must be dealt with in another manner. TOD only takes affect at your death. As with a Will, TOD will not help you if you become incapacitated. Also, the entire account is distributed outright upon your death. If you have minor children or beneficiaries who, for one reason or another, cannot manage money, and you want to have the money managed for their benefit, you should not use a TOD.

"In Trust For" "In Trust For" designations at banks and other financial institutions are similar to TOD accounts in that you can name a person or persons to receive the funds in your account after your death and avoid probate. This designation is generally used for checking account, savings accounts and certificates of deposit. The "In Trust For" designation has the same advantages and disadvantages as Transfer on Death.

Joint Ownership. It is very common in Florida for a surviving spouse to add the name of a child to a deed or to an account or other asset in order to avoid probate. If the ownership is created properly and provides that the property is owned as "joint tenants with right of survivorship," then the asset will pass to the survivor upon the first to die. Although this method avoids probate, it may cause more problems than it solves.

Gift Tax. The addition of your child's name on the asset is a transfer of at least half of the property by gift. It may be subject to gift tax if it is large enough. Also the gift does not provide a "stepped-up basis" to your child for tax purposes. If your child would have received the ownership of the asset as a result of your death, then his or her "basis" in the property would be the value of the property at your death. The basis is "stepped-up" from your basis in the property (the value at the time you acquired it plus any capital improvements you made to the asset). However, because your child received the property as a result of a gift, he or she will also acquire your basis in the property. If the property has increased in value during your ownership, this will mean that your child will realize a greater capital gain as a result of the gift and increased capital gains taxes.

As an example, Mr. Smith purchased a rental property in 1980 for $60,000. In 2003, Mr. Smith wants to add his daughter to the title to avoid probate. The day after adding his daughter, Mr. Smith dies. The property is worth $200,000. Mr. Smith's daughter receives the property without probate and immediately sells it for $200,000. Since she received the property as a gift, her basis is the same as her father's, $60,000. Therefore her capital gain is $140,000 which, at a 15% capital gains tax rate, incurs $21,000 in taxes. If Mr. Smith would have transferred the property to a revocable Trust and named his daughter as the beneficiary of the rental property, she would have received the property without probate, her basis would have been the value at the time of her father's death, $200,000. She would have no capital gain and no taxes as a result of the sale.

Liability. By putting your daughter's name on the asset, you have added her liabilities to the property. If your daughter is in an automobile accident, is sued as a result and has a judgment entered against her, that judgment can become a lien against your property. Her creditors may be able to attach the jointly held property as a means of satisfying her debt. This also applies to bank and investment accounts.

Loss of Control. Also, if your daughter is joint tenant on a parcel of real estate, you cannot sell the property or even put a mortgage on it without her approval and joinder on the deed or mortgage. Even worse, if the jointly held asset is a bank account or investment account, she may be able to sell, liquidate or transfer the asset without your approval or even without your knowledge. You're saying, "I trust my daughter. I know she would completely cooperate with my wishes and wouldn't do anything that was not in my best interest." While this may be true, consider what would happen if your daughter gets a divorce or becomes incapacitated. Would her ex-husband claim any interest in your property? Who would be appointed as her guardian or have authority to act in her behalf if she was unable?

Loss of Homestead. If the property you are adding your daughter's name to is homestead, the change in title may cause you to lose at least a part of your homestead exemption, and would cause your property to be revalued for property tax purposes and cause you to lose the advantage of the "Save Our

Homes" Amendment. Depending on how long you have owned your home, it could cause your property taxes to double and possibly even triple.

These disadvantages only apply if you are adding someone other than your spouse to your title. Property owned by husband and wife (or as tenants by the entireties) would be treated completely different than the examples described above. Property owned as tenants by the entirety cannot be attached by creditors of only one spouse. The creditor must have a claim or judgment against both spouses. Adding a spouse to homestead property will not cause a loss in the homestead exemption nor will it affect the value under the "Save Our Homes" Amendment. We will discuss these issues in the chapter on Homestead.

No Survivor. Finally, if both joint tenants die in a common accident, there is no survivor to maintain title to the property. The property will, in that case, go through probate.

Annuities, IRAs and Life Insurance. Annuities, Individual Retirement Accounts, life insurance policies, pension plans and other retirement plans provide that the owner may name beneficiaries who would receive the proceeds of the asset upon the death of the owner. The transfers to the beneficiaries would be paid by contract and avoid probate. Most of these assets will also allow you to name a contingent beneficiary if the primary beneficiary named does not survive you. If none of the beneficiaries that you name survive you, then the proceeds will be paid to your probate estate.

It is extremely important that you routinely review the beneficiary designations to your life insurance policies, annuities and retirement accounts. The death of named beneficiaries or changes in your life circumstances could render old beneficiary designations worthless or worse.

Naming Beneficiaries for Your Individual Retirement Account. Naming a beneficiary to your Individual Retirement Account (IRA) can be one of the most important aspects to your estate planning. An IRA is a retirement tool that allow the earnings from the assets contained within it to grow tax deferred. That means that any income generated within the IRA is not taxable until the owner takes the earnings out of the IRA. This greatly helps the assets within the IRA grow at a much higher rate than investments whose earnings are taxed each year.

A traditional IRA can be funded with pre-tax money and you receive an annual income tax deduction, up to certain limits, when you contribute money to the IRA. The assets can be left in the IRA, with the earnings tax deferred, until you are required to start taking distributions from it. Some persons who do not need to tap into their IRA for living expenses can extend the tax deferral and, with proper estate planning, can pass these savings and continued deferral on to their heirs.

Naming A Beneficiary After The Death Of The Owner. First of all, it is important to know that you can and should name a beneficiary or beneficiaries to your IRA. Failure to do so will result in your IRA being distributed to the IRA Custodian's default beneficiary. This is usually your probate estate.

That means that your IRA assets will need to go through probate to get to the ultimate beneficiaries. This will cost you likely thousands of dollars of probate expenses, months of administration time and can limit the distribution alternatives for the beneficiaries. For example, you may lose any of the following powerful estate planning tools:

- The spousal "roll over" provision.
- The ability of your beneficiaries to take distributions over their life expectancy.
- All of these could result in higher income tax rates and possible penalties.

Minimum Distribution Rules For Beneficiaries. IRAs are subject to required minimum distribution rules to the beneficiaries after the death of the IRA owner. How and when the distributions must occur after a death depends on a number of factors including who the owner names as primary beneficiary and contingent (or backup) beneficiaries, and whether the owner dies before or after he or she begins taking lifetime required minimum distributions.

If the IRA owner has named someone other than his or her spouse as beneficiary, the beneficiary may have a few options upon the death of the owner . One of these options will generally be to take annual distributions over a fixed period of time based on the beneficiary's life expectancy at the time of the IRA owner's death (in some cases the period of time can be based on the remaining life expectancy of the IRA owner, if this results in a longer period of time). Young beneficiaries with long life expectancies can spread distributions over a substantial period of time, keeping the maximum amount allowable in the tax-deferred IRA.

If the IRA owner has named his or her spouse as beneficiary, then the spouse has additional options upon the death of the owner. A surviving spouse will commonly opt to roll over inherited IRA funds into his or her own IRA. Or, if your surviving spouse is your sole beneficiary, he or she may opt to simply leave the funds in an inherited IRA and treat that IRA as his or her own. With either of these options, the surviving spouse names his or her own beneficiaries. At some point, the spouse is required to begin taking lifetime required minimum distributions. When the spouse dies, the beneficiary has the option to take distributions based on his or her life expectancy.

You also have the option of naming a revocable trust as your IRA beneficiary. Many persons are concerned that their children may not appreciate the value of tax-deferral and may cash in the IRA in one big lump distribution. This will usually result in needless taxes and penalties. By naming your trust as beneficiary you can retain some control as to how distributions will be taken after your death. In some cases, a trust may not have the advantages of an individual to "stretch" out the distributions, so you will have to weigh the pros and cons of this method.

As you can see, there are many options for designating beneficiaries for your IRA. It is well worth the time and effort to research your alternatives and name primary and contingent beneficiaries.

The Enhanced Life Estate Deed. For persons trying to pass their property to their heirs without going through probate and without setting up a trust, a problem area has always been real estate. You can add a transfer on death designation to your bank and investment accounts and maintain full ownership of those accounts until your death. At that time the accounts would be paid directly to your designated "beneficiary" without probate.

Real estate presented more of a problem. A person (called the "Grantor") could transfer their property to their children (or anyone else) and retain a "life estate" in the property. Under this arrangement, the Grantor would own the property, with full right of occupancy for her lifetime and at the time of her death, it would pass, free of probate, to the children (or other persons) named as the "remaindermen."

The big problem with this arrangement would arise when the Grantor wanted to sell the property during her lifetime. Since she had transferred the interest in the property that existed after her death, she could only sell her life estate. This meant that the buyer would only own the property until the Grantor's death. At that time title would automatically revert to the remaindermen. It's easy to see why no one would want to buy from the Grantor under those circumstances. In order to give the buyer full fee simple title to the property, the remaindermen would also have to sign the deed.

Florida has a solution to this problem. It's called the Enhanced Life Estate deed. An Enhanced Life Estate deed allows the Grantor to retain a life estate with complete control over the property. She has no obligations to the remaindermen and does not need their consent to sell, mortgage, gift or otherwise transfer the ownership of the property. That is where the "enhanced" feature comes in.

The remainder beneficiary of an Enhanced Life Estate has no vested ownership interest prior to the Grantor's death and in the case of homestead property, it would not cause any revaluation of the Florida save our homes exemption for property tax purposes. It is not a completed gift until the moment of death and would therefore get a step up in basis for capital gains at the date of death.

Advantages Of The Enhanced Life Estate Deed

- Allows you to pass your real estate at death without probate.
- Does not affect the homestead status of the property

- Does not require lender approval or condominium or homeowner association approval
- You will not be required to file a gift tax return since IRS considers the transfer and incomplete gift
- The value of the interest transferred will not be considered as a completed gift for Medicaid purposes and will not be the basis for a "waiting period" that could delay your access to Medicaid benefits to pay for skilled nursing home care.

Disadvantages Of The Enhanced LifeEstate Deed

- At your death, the title goes directly to the remainder beneficiaries. If one or more have judgment liens against them, the lien will immediately attach to the property.
- There is no central "trustee" who can sell the property on behalf of the other remainder beneficiaries. All of the remainder beneficiaries will be required to consent to the terms of the sale.
- If a remainder beneficiary is unable to manage his or her affairs, a guardian may have to be appointed to deal with the property.

The Revocable Trust

The Revocable Trust. The mechanism for avoiding probate that offers the most flexibility is the revocable Trust. A Trust is a legal arrangement in which one party holds the property of another party for the benefit of a third party. While this definition may not make a whole lot of sense to you now, we will revisit it when we discuss how the Trust works. Quite simply, when you set up a Trust for estate planning purposes, you create an entity that will own your property. Because your property is now owned by this entity and not you, when you die or become incapacitated, there is no estate to probate. All of the property remains in the Trust and will be managed or distributed according to the terms of the Trust.

Even though you no longer own the property individually, you will have complete control over the property in the Trust. In fact, overall you will have a greater control because the property will not come under the control of a court appointed personal representative or guardian at the time of your death or incapacity.

Probably the easiest way to describe how a Trust works is to talk about the different persons involved in the Trust. Let's look back to our initial definition of a Trust. "A legal arrangement in which one party holds the property of another party for the benefit of a third party." If we insert the terms of each of the parties it would look like this: "A legal arrangement in which *a Trustee* holds the property of *a Grantor* for the benefit of *a Beneficiary.*"

The first person involved in the Trust that we will discuss is the Grantor. The Grantor is the creator of the Trust. You are the Grantor of your Trust. As the Grantor, you have the right to set up the Trust as you wish. You will determine who will manage the Trust, how the Trust property will be administered and to whom the property will ultimately be distributed. As Grantor, you also have the right to make changes or amendments to the Trust. If circumstances change in the future or if you just change your mind about some provision of the Trust, you can amend it. You can even go as far as revoking the Trust in its entirety. The Grantor is the only person who can amend the Trust. Upon your death, no one else can make changes to the Trust and your wishes must be carried out.

The second person involved in the Trust is the Trustee. The Trustee is the person who manages or administers the Trust. In most cases you will also be the Trustee of the Trust. Therefore as Grantor, you have complete control over the terms and provisions of the Trust, and as the Trustee you control the management of the property in the Trust. As a result you will probably not notice any difference in dealing with your assets within the Trust than before you set up the Trust. You will have complete control of your assets and will not be restricted in what you can do with them.

If you should become incapacitated or upon your death, a Successor Trustee, who you have selected, will step up and manage the Trust assets in your place. You can appoint almost anyone you wish to serve as your Successor Trustee. It can be a spouse, relative, friend or trust company. You would appoint the Successor Trustee at the time you create and execute the Trust. The Successor Trustee would, at the time of your incapacity, resignation or death, have the authority to manage the Trust assets pursuant to the terms of the Trust.

If your Successor Trustee steps up as a result of your incapacity, he would make sure that your investments are properly managed, that your other assets are cared for, that your bills are paid and that you are cared for in the manner that is necessary and customary to meet your needs. The Successor Trustee cannot take any of your property or income for his own benefit unless you authorize it or it is specifically authorized in the Trust.

If the Successor Trustee takes over as a result of your death, he would manage and distribute the property in the Trust according to the instructions set forth in the Trust. The Trustee is the holder of legal title to the assets that you put into the Trust. If Trust property is to be sold, purchased, encumbered or given away, the Trustee is the one who executes these transactions.

The third person involved in the Trust is the Beneficiary. As the name indicates, the Beneficiary is the person (or persons) who receives the benefits of the Trust. During your lifetime, you will be the Beneficiary of your Trust. All income that is earned by the assets of the Trust (such as dividends from stocks, interest from bonds and certificates of deposit and rent from real estate) is available to you to do as you please. You may spend this income, invest it or even give it away. Again the Trust does not create any restrictions. You will also pay tax on the income just as you did prior to creating the Trust. A revocable Trust will have no effect on your income taxes. Since the taxpayer identification number of the Trust is your social security number and all income is reported under it, the IRS won't even know that you have a Trust. And, believe it or not, they won't even care.

At the time of your death, the beneficiaries then become those persons to whom you have designated your estate to be distributed. Your Trust provisions can specify that your beneficiaries receive their share outright or it can be held in trust for them. The method of distribution you decide can be extremely flexible. If a beneficiary's share is held in trust, the Trustee will manage and invest the assets and distribute them according to the terms of the Trust. You may direct that only income from the share be paid to the beneficiary, or that principal installments be paid on certain dates, or that the beneficiary receive the share upon reaching a certain age or upon a certain event such as marriage, graduation from college or entering into a business. You can make the distribution provisions very strict or you may give the Trustee a large amount of discretion.

The Trust can also contain provisions regarding distribution to a contingent beneficiary in cases where the primary beneficiary predeceases the Grantor. For example, you may want to leave a portion of your estate to your brother, but you can provide that, if your brother does not survive you, his share will be distributed among his children. You can also specify that, if his children are minors or incapacitated, the Trustee will hold their shares until they reach a certain age at which time it will be distributed to them. If your brother survives you, then he will receive his entire share.

Estate Tax Savings. A revocable Trust can also be used to eliminate or minimize the amount of estate tax that will be due upon your death. The Internal Revenue Code states that, in 2013, any individual may pass $5,120,000 to his heirs without any estate tax due. This credit against estate tax is called the unified credit. In addition, if you are married when you die, you can take advantage of the unlimited marital deduction. This means that you can leave as much of your estate to your spouse, outright or in trust, and it will not be subject to federal estate tax. If you leave it to your spouse in trust, the only requirement is that you must give your spouse the right to all of the income generated by the property.

By combining the unified credit with the unlimited marital deduction, it is possible for a married couple to leave $10,240,000 to their heirs without estate taxes.

Let's take the case of Homer and Marge. Homer and Marge are both in their second marriage. Homer came into the marriage with $3 million in assets and Marge brought $6 million. The two have agreed that after they have both passed away, they want Homer's children to receive $3 million and Marge's children to get $6 million. Marge wants to provide for Homer if she should die first, but still wants her children to receive the $6 million after his death. And neither wants to pay any federal estate tax.

To accomplish this, Homer and Marge had their estate planning attorney create a revocable Trust for each of them. The Trust provided that upon the death of one, if the spouse survived, an amount of the deceased spouse's estate equal to the unified credit would be set aside in a trust called the "credit shelter" trust. The remaining amount, if any, would be held in a second trust called the "marital deduction" trust. The Trust document provided that all income from both trusts would be paid to the surviving spouse for his or her lifetime and, upon the death of the surviving spouse, it would be distributed to the first deceased spouse's children.

In November, 2013, Marge died. The figure below shows how the property was distributed pursuant to Wilma's Trust agreement.

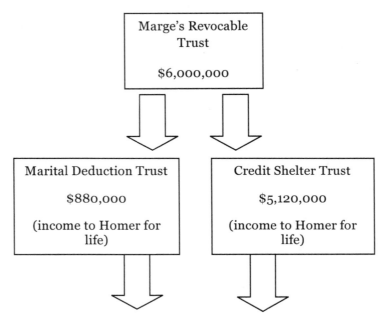

After Homer's death, all property in both trusts distributed to Marge's children

At Marge's death, an amount equal to the full unified credit ($5,120,000) was distributed to the

Credit Shelter Trust. This amount was held for Homer's benefit but did not become a part of Homer's estate. It passed into the Credit Shelter Trust free of estate tax because it did not exceed the unified credit amount.

The remaining amount in Marge's revocable Trust ($880,000) passed into the Marital Deduction Trust. There was no estate tax on this amount because it was a transfer to a surviving spouse and, because of the unlimited marital deduction, was not subject to estate taxes. It qualified for the marital deduction even though Homer could not touch the principal amount, because Homer was entitled to all of the income generated by the property in the Marital Deduction Trust.

During the remainder of his life, Homer received the income from both trusts and thus received the support that they both wanted. Upon Homer's death, the principal in both trusts passed to Marge's children free of estate tax. The property in the Credit Shelter Trust was not taxed because it was not greater than the unified credit amount in effect at the time of Marge's death. Even if the amount in the Credit Shelter Trust had increased to $10 million dollars, Marge's children would have received it free of estate taxes. There would however, have been capital gains taxes due in that situation. The property in the Marital Deduction Trust passed to Marge's children free of estate taxes because it became a part of Homer's estate and, combined with the value of the property Homer owned outright ($3,000,000), did not exceed the unified credit.

Because Homer and Marge properly planned their estate, they were able to pass their assets to their children according to their wishes and without incurring any estate taxes.

Funding the Trust. The revocable Trust is a powerful and efficient estate planning tool to avoid probate and reduce estate taxes. However, it is important to understand that the Trust is only effective for those assets that have been transferred to the Trust. You can pay a fortune for a terrific Trust agreement, but if your assets are not titled in the name of the Trust, they will still have to pass through probate to get to your heirs.

I frequently meet with new clients who have had their trust prepared elsewhere and want me to review their estate plan. The come into my office with a big, leather bound binder. The office lights reflect off of the gold lettering that majestically says: "Estate Plan." Before I even open the binder, I ask my new clients, "Have you funded the trust?" They look at me like I'm from Mars. They have no idea what I'm talking about. They also have no idea that the plan

50

they paid thousands of dollars for will cause all of their assets to go through probate. That is, until we properly fund the trust.

The first step in funding the Trust is determining the correct name in which to title your assets. The property will not be owned by the Trust itself but by the Trustee, subject to the terms of the Trust. The proper way to designate ownership is:

John Smith, Trustee of the John Smith Trust dated July 4, 2013.

Any assets transferred to the Trust should be titled in this name. Deeds must be prepared to transfer real estate from the Grantor to the Trustee. Because of Florida's unique laws, transferring homestead to your Trust **improperly** may create serious title problems. You should consult with a competent estate planning attorney before doing so. Bank accounts should be titled in the name of the Trustee, as should stocks, bonds and mutual funds. However, individual retirement accounts, 401(k) plans, certain annuity contracts and other tax deferred investments will usually remain in the name of the Grantor. Transferring these investments into the Trust may have adverse tax consequences.

Regarding life insurance, you should consider having your spouse as primary beneficiary of the insurance policy on your life and vice versa, and that the Trustee be named as a contingent beneficiary using the following designation: *Successor Trustee of the John Smith Trust dated July 4, 2013.* You should contact your insurance agent and request him or her to provide you with the necessary forms to change ownership of the policies and to make the change of beneficiary as indicated.

Before naming the Trustee as beneficiary of any tax deferred investment, you should consult with your tax advisor. There may be tax advantages to naming individuals as beneficiaries as opposed to a trust.

Remember, if you do not transfer your assets to your Trust, it will do you no good in your goal to avoid probate. Any assets owned individually by you at the time of your death that do not have transfer on death or beneficiary designations will have to go through probate to get to your Trust and eventually to your heirs.

Choosing a Trustee. One of the aspects of setting up a revocable trust that cannot be taken too lightly is the choice of a successor trustee. In most cases you are the trustee of your revocable trust during your lifetime. This gives you the authority to manage your assets in the same manner as you did before setting up the trust. However, if you should become incapacitated or upon your death, another person appointed by you will take over the management of the trust. This is the successor trustee.

If the successor trustee takes over as a result of your incapacity, he or she will manage your finances, pay your bills and make sure you are taken care of financially. If the successor trustee takes over as a result of your death, he or she will distribute the trust assets in accordance with your wishes as stated in the trust agreement. Depending on the terms of your trust, the successor trustee may have a great deal of discretion in determining how the assets are invested and distributed.

For this reason, the selection of your successor trustee should be a serious, well thought-out decision. The following issues are considerations that should be made in selecting your trustee.

1. The successor trustee should be familiar with you and your wishes regarding how your assets should be managed, invested and distributed. At times a successor trustee will have discretion as to whether or not to distribute assets to a particular beneficiary. The beneficiary may need money for education, may not be good a managing money or

may have special needs. The successor trustee should be familiar with these circumstances and know what your wishes are regarding them.

2. The successor trustee should be a responsible person that you have confidence in. For this reason, many people choose spouses, adult children or other family members or close friends. The factor of trust is usually more important than their knowledge since the successor trustee can rely on an attorney and accountant to help them administer the trust.

3. The successor trustee must be agreeable with the appointment. Some people do not want the responsibility of serving as a trustee. You should discuss in detail the duties, responsibilities and expectations with your successor trustee before naming him or her.

4. You may want to consider naming more than one person as your successor trustee. Many people name two or more of their children as co-successor trustees. This has the benefit of taking advantage of each child's strengths. It also eliminates the perception of showing favoritism to one child over another. The disadvantage of naming more than one trustee to act together is ..... they must agree and act together. If you select two persons who have a

history of not being able to work together, the position of trustee usually magnifies this problem.

5. If you cannot come up with an individual to serve as trustee, you may wish to consider a corporate trustee. Many banks and investment companies have trust departments that specialize in serving as trustees of trusts. The advantages include the expertise and knowledge they have in administering trusts and estates, the fact that they can act in an unbiased manner (family politics will not affect the management and distribution of the trust), and the fact that they are bonded and insured. Disadvantages of corporate trustee are the fees (they are usually higher than those paid to a family member) and the fact that they don't know your family's dynamic. Further, some corporate trustees require a minimum estate size in order to serve.

You should also consider naming a back-up or more than one back-up to your successor trustee. If the person you have chosen as your successor trustee dies before you, becomes incapacitated or moves away, you should have someone you trust to step in and serve.

Amending the Trust. One of the most advantageous characteristics of a revocable trust is its flexibility. The Grantor, or creator, of the trust has the authority to amend the trust at any time. So if the law changes or circumstances in your life change, or you simply change your mind, you can change any provisions of the trust. This includes revoking the trust in its entirety if you wish.

If the trust is a joint revocable trust created by a husband and wife, and one of the spouses dies, the survivor can usually continue to amend the trust -- unless there is a specific provision in the trust prohibiting it.

When amending the trust, your attorney will prepare an amendment which only affects the part of the trust you wish to change. The entire document does not need to be redone. That being said, in some cases, after a number of amendments, you may wish to restate the trust to make it less cumbersome and easier to comprehend. In this case, the new restated document is still the same trust for the purpose of titling assets. You will not need to retitle your assets into a new trust name.

Many people make the mistake of crossing out a provision of their trust, writing in the changes and initialling the change. DON'T DO THIS. This will not effectively amend the trust and may even invalidate all or a part of the trust. Florida law requires that a trust document and any amendments to it be executed by the Grantor(s) in the presence of two witnesses who must also execute the document.

Marking up the existing trust and initialing it does not comply with this requirement.

It is also important to know that only the Grantor can amend the trust. If the Grantor has died or is incompetent, the trust may not be amended. Also, an attorney-in-fact under the Grantor's durable power of attorney cannot amend the trust on behalf of the Grantor. This is to ensure that the Grantor's wishes be carried out and not unilaterally be changed by some other person.

Other Documents in Your Estate Plan

The Revocable Trust is just the centerpiece of your estate plan. It is important to have other documents that address issues that the Trust cannot or was not intended to address. The documents make sure that you are covered for any estate planning situation.

Pour-Over Wills. Even though you have prepared a Trust and transferred all of your assets into it, you still need a Will. No matter how careful and diligent you are in funding your Trust, it is always possible that you may forget to put an asset into it. It is also possible for you (your estate) to acquire property after your death such as an insurance settlement or an inheritance that you became entitled to during your lifetime but was not actually distributed until after the time of your death.

In these cases, the only way to get these assets to your heirs is through probate. A Pour-Over Will is similar to the Wills we discussed earlier; however, its purpose is to take any property not in your Trust at the time of your death and transfer or "pour it over" into the Trust. This requires the property to go through probate, so the Pour-Over Will is only used as a last resort or safety net. In the vast majority of well planned estates, it is never used.

Durable Power of Attorney. No one likes to think about becoming incapable of handling their own affairs. Yet, the durable power of attorney has always been an important part of an individual's estate planning arsenal. This document provides a means for you to appoint another person (usually your spouse, another family member or a close trusted friend) to handle your financial affairs and manage your assets and property when you are unable to do so yourself. The term "durable" shows your intent that the other person, called an attorney-in-fact, will have authority to act for you even if you are incapacitated.

The durable power of attorney must be in writing and must also be signed by two witnesses. The attorney-in-fact may be a spouse, relative, friend or almost anyone you choose, provided that person is 18 or older and of sound mind. The durable power of attorney is valid from the time you sign it until such time as you revoke it, you are declared incompetent by a court, or upon your death.

The importance of a durable power of attorney becomes evident when you consider the alternatives. If you became incapacitated without a durable power of attorney, a court would have to appoint a guardian to manage your affairs, pay your bills and maintain your property and investments. Guardianship proceedings can be time consuming and expensive and there is no guarantee that the court will appoint the person you would have wanted as guardian. You can easily avoid this situation if you plan and appoint an attorney- in-fact to act on your behalf.

With a well drafted durable power of attorney, your attorney-in-fact will be able to make decisions about your property on your behalf. He or she would be able to sign checks to pay your bills and medical expenses, oversee and direct your investments, sign deeds and enter into contracts on your behalf. Of course you can structure the durable power of attorney to restrict or eliminate any of these powers. That way you can provide for your incapacity without giving up control of your assets. Under no circumstance can an attorney-in-fact change your will, exercise personal services, or vote in any public election on your behalf.

Even if you have set up a revocable trust, the durable power of attorney is an important element of your estate planning. The primary reason most people set up trusts is to avoid probate; however, only assets that are properly transferred into trust ownership will escape probate administration. Therefore, if you become incapacitated and your family discovers that you forgot to transfer shares of stock into the trust, those shares would be subject to probate at the time of your death. If you had executed a power of attorney with specific authority to transfer assets to your trust, your attorney-in-fact could put the stock into trust ownership prior to your death, thereby saving your heirs the time and expense of probate administration.

Also, as we discussed earlier, IRAs are not transferred into your revocable trust. Therefore the Trustee has no authority over them. If you needed to take a distribution from your IRA and were incapacitated or otherwise unable to authorize such transaction, the attorney-in-fact named in your

Durable Power of Attorney would be able to direct the distribution.

In 2011, the Florida Legislature passed a revised bill which the Governor signed into law which drastically changed the durable power of attorney in Florida. The law took effect on October 1, 2011 and applies to all durable powers of attorney created after that date. Powers of attorney that were created and signed prior to October 1, 2011, are still valid but are not interpreted the same as the new ones.

Some of the highlights of the new law are:

1. Certain sweeping powers granted to an attorney-in-fact - so-called "superpowers" - require special treatment. One example of a superpower is the ability to make gifts from the principal's funds. To grant an attorney-in-fact the ability to exercise a superpower, that superpower must be specifically mentioned in the durable power of attorney, and that section of the document physically initialed by the principal.

2. If the principal desires that co-attorneys-in-fact act only with the knowledge and consent of the others, the durable power of attorney must specifically say so. If this provision is not included in the durable power of attorney, it is assumed that each co-attorney-in-fact may act independently, without the knowledge or consent of the others.

3. The new law also states that banks and financial institutions must honor a photocopy or electronic copy of the signed durable power of attorney. Again this only applies to the new form.

4. The "springing" power of attorney, where the attorney-in-fact only has authority after a doctor certifies that the principal is incapacitated, is abolished. All attorneys-in-fact now have authority to act as soon as the document is executed.

These are only a few of the changes in the law. If you have a power of attorney that is dated prior to October 1, 2011, we recommend that you contact an estate planning attorney to have your document reviewed and possibly revised.

Advanced Health Care Directives. The 2005 Terri Schiavo case thrust Florida into the forefront in the national debate about health care decision making and whether a person has a right to refuse medical care and treatment.

Terri Schiavo was a young woman who had a heart attack which severely damaged her brain, including her cerebral cortex which controls her conscious thought. Many doctors concluded that Terri's condition was a persistent vegetative state and she was institutionalized for 15 years until her death. In 1988, her husband and court appointed guardian, Michael Schiavo, petitioned the Pinellas County

Circuit Court to remove her feeding tube. He claimed that she had confided to him verbally that she would not want to be kept alive by artificial means. Terri's parents, Robert and Mary Schindler opposed this, saying that such a statement would be completely out of character for her and that she believed in the sanctity of life.

The court battle continued for 7 years and included 14 appeals in the Florida courts and 5 actions in Federal District Court. The Florida legislature passed a law, called "Terri's Law," which allowed Governor Jeb Bush to order her feeding tube reinserted. The Florida Supreme Court overturned the law and the United States Supreme Court four times refused to consider the case. Congress even tried to call for hearings on the matter under which they subpoenaed Terri and Michael Schiavo to testify. Celebrities, politicians and advocacy groups publicly argued the issues of the case. The saga was played out on television and radio talk shows across the nation and it seemed everyone had an opinion about how Terri Schiavo should be treated medically.

Finally, on March 18, 2005, Circuit Court judge ordered Terri's feeding tube removed. After a flurry of last minute petitions and appeals, Terri Schiavo died on March 25, 2005, 15 years and one month after collapsing in her home. The debate still rages.

A sad but interesting fact is that all of this could have been avoided had Terri Schiavo made and executed a valid living will.

The two types of Advance Directives in Florida are the Designation of Health Care Surrogate and the Living Will.

Designation of Health Care Surrogate. Simply speaking, a Designation of Health Care Surrogate is a written document designating a person or surrogate to make health care decisions on your behalf. The document must be signed by the you (or you must direct someone to sign for you) in the presence of two separate witnesses who must also sign the document. The surrogate named in the document cannot serve as a witness.

The surrogate does not have any authority to make decisions on your behalf until it has been determined by your attending physician that you are physically or mentally unable to communicate a willful and knowing health care decision. This determination must then be corroborated by a second physician. If both physicians find that you cannot make health care decisions, they record that fact in your medical record and notify the surrogate in writing that he or she has authority to make the decisions.

Once the surrogate obtains authority to act, he or she is responsible to act for you and make all health care decisions during your incapacity in accordance with your instructions. The last phrase is why it is important that you carefully consider your wishes, put them in writing and discuss them with the surrogate and with your family.

Living Will. A Living Will in Florida is a written declaration which states your intentions if you should be in a terminal condition, have an end-stage condition or are in a persistent vegetative state with no hope of recovery. Using this document you would direct whether you wanted life-prolonging procedures provided, withheld or withdrawn.

A "terminal condition" is defined under the Florida Statutes as a condition caused by injury, disease or illness from which there is no reasonable medical probability of recovery and which, without treatment, can be expected to cause death.

An "end-stage condition" means an irreversible condition that is caused by injury, disease or illness which has resulted in progressively severe and permanent deterioration, and which treatment, to a reasonable degree of medical probability, would be ineffective.

A "persistent vegetative state" is a permanent and irreversible condition of unconsciousness in which there is (a) the absence of voluntary action or cognitive behavior of any kind and (b) an inability to communicate or interact purposefully with the environment.

In determining your condition, your attending or treating physician and at least one other consulting physician must separately examine you. Both physicians must find that you suffer from one of the above conditions before life-prolonging procedures may be withheld or withdrawn.

A Living Will must be signed by you, or someone else at your direction, in the presence of two witnesses who must also sign the document. One of the witnesses has to be someone other than your spouse or blood relative. You may designate a surrogate to carry out your wishes, but the failure to do so will not make the Living Will invalid.

The law makes it your responsibility to notify your attending physician that the Living Will has been signed. For this reason, it is important that you bring the signed Living Will to your doctor as soon as possible after you have signed it. The doctor can make a copy to put into your medical records.

No one wants to be in the position Terri Schiavo and her family found themselves. Make it a point to speak to your attorney or health care provider about advanced directives and healthcare decision making.

Conclusion. There is no "one size fits all" solution to estate planning. Every person has different objectives, assets and family circumstances. There are many ways to pass your estate to your heirs. Even a total absence of planning will result in the distribution of your estate. However, if you are concerned about avoiding probate, minimizing taxes, maintaining privacy and reducing administration costs, you must pro-actively plan your estate.

Estate Planning Lessons From the Sopranos. When James Gandolfini died in June of 2013, the popularity of the Sopranos star led to intense public scrutiny. Initially, the attention centered on his death, then his career, followed by his lifestyle and eating habits. Now, believe it or not, his estate planning is the target of fascination.

Since the probate process is a court proceeding open to the public, reporters and pundits have poured through Mr. Gandolfini's estate files. They have discovered, and it has been made public, that he prepared a simple Will to guide the administration of a large and complex estate.

This has led to criticism of his method of estate planning. Columnists and legal experts have denounced the use of this simple Will. They claim that it has caused his estate to incur unnecessary estate taxes, that it does not provide adequately for his son and that it has led to wasteful probate expenses and painful publicity for his family. (The reporters' own articles proved that last point.)

Mr. Gandolfini's estate planning attorney insists that these accounts are inaccurate and do not tell the whole story. Mr. Gandolfini, he claims, had a thorough gifting program and used irrevocable trusts and other instruments to minimize estate taxes and provide for efficient administration of his estate.

Whether Mr. Gandolfini's estate plan is sound may never be known to the public. The point of this article is that all of the scrutiny and resulting pain to his family could have easily been avoided.

Had Mr. Gandolfini used a revocable trust rather than the simple Will, the administration and distribution of those assets would have remained private. Since assets placed in a revocable trust avoid probate, the trust's terms and contents are not a matter of public record. In the unlikely event that the use of a Will was necessary to transfer assets, it would have been a pour-over Will leaving everything to the privately administered trust.

While you may not be a famous Hollywood actor whose private life is hounded by the media, you probably would not like your financial affairs open to the public's (this means business associates or rivals, neighbors, and certain family members) prying eyes.

72

Issues Unique to Florida

Homestead and Estate Planning

Florida places restrictions on how a person can leave his homestead property after his death if he is survived by a spouse or minor child. This is important for estate planning purposes because failure to heed these restrictions can result in an ownership nightmare.

This is why I recommend that you do **not** use one of those fill in the blanks wills or trusts that you can purchase from an office supply store or on the internet. You may save some money, but as you're going to see, your family may pay dearly for years to come.

What happens to your homestead after your death centers on three different issues: 1) is the property your homestead? 2) how does the homestead pass to your next generation? and 3) is the homestead free from the claims of your creditors?

Is It Homestead Property? Before we can plan the distribution of your homestead, we must determine whether the property is homestead at the time of death. Florida law defines homestead as real property, of no more than 160 contiguous acres outside a municipality, or no more than one half an acre of contiguous land in a municipality and the house and other improvements on it, owned by a natural person who is a Florida resident. The property must be the owner's principal residence.

If the property meets these qualifications the homestead law applies. If not, then the property is treated the same as any other asset in your estate. In probate proceedings your personal representative (or executor) can ask the court to determine if the property is homestead.

Legal Restrictions. If you are married, the Florida Constitution does not allow you to leave your homestead to anyone other than your surviving spouse. If you have a minor child, things get really complicated. Therefore, how you can dispose of your homestead in your will is dependent on whether or not you are married or have a minor child at the time of death. If you are not survived by a spouse or minor child, you may devise the property in any manner you wish. The term devise means transfer according to the terms of a will or trust. If you have a spouse but no minor child, you may devise the homestead only to your spouse. In addition, the devise to your spouse must be of your entire interest in the homestead property. If you have a minor child, you cannot devise the homestead property at all. In this situation, as I explain below, the homestead should be owned by the husband and wife as tenants by the entirety.

The next obvious question is: What happens if the owner tries to devise the homestead other than allowed?

If you are survived by a spouse and have a provision in your will or trust which tries to leave the homestead to anyone other than your surviving spouse, the provisions of the will are disregarded by law, your spouse takes a life estate (she owns the property for a term ending at the time of her death) in the homestead, with a vested remainder to your lineal descendants (at the death of your spouse, title to the homestead immediately passes to your children who were alive at the date of your death).

Under these circumstances your surviving spouse only has ownership for the remainder of her life. As a result she can only transfer the same interest to a third party.

For example, if your surviving spouse sells her interest in the homestead to her friend and dies a week later, the friend's interest would terminate at your spouse's death and title would pass to your lineal descendants. This creates the unintended situation where the surviving spouse must obtain the consent of your lineal descendants if she wishes to sell or mortgage the homestead. If you would have left his entire interest in the homestead to your surviving spouse, then the surviving spouse would not have a life estate but full fee simple title with authority to sell and mortgage as she pleased.

If husband and wife own the homestead property together as tenants by the entireties, the restrictions do not apply, and upon the death of one, the surviving spouse has full interest in the property.

This is the case even when there is a minor child. For this reason, married couples with a minor child should almost always own their homestead as husband and wife, as tenants by the entireties.

Claims of Creditors. Upon your death, the assets of your probate estate are used to pay any debts that you owed at the time of death, as well as expenses of administration. The probate estate generally consists of assets in your sole name, which contain no provision for automatic succession of ownership at death (such as beneficiary designations). This includes personal property owned by you wherever located and real estate located in Florida, except homestead.

The Florida Constitution provides that your spouse or heirs benefit from the homestead exemption. In other words, your exemption from forced sale by creditors passes to your surviving spouse or heirs. The term "heirs" in this context means those persons who would take your property if you died intestate (without a will). These are usually your lineal descendants such as children and grandchildren.

Therefore, if you devise your homestead to your spouse or to your heirs that would receive it had there been no will, then your creditors cannot reach the homestead and the property passes "free of the claims of creditors."

If the homestead is devised to persons other than your surviving spouse or heirs (such as a good friend), it is subject to the claims of creditors and is treated as a part of the probate estate.

If you direct in your will that the homestead be sold and the proceeds distributed, then the proceeds are not exempt from the claims of your creditors, even if such proceeds would be distributed to your heirs.

Proper estate planning in Florida must take the strange and unique homestead laws of Florida into account. Distributions that neglect to consider these laws can cause a family to lose one of its most valued and treasured assets -- your home.

Tenancy By The Entireties.

Florida is one of a handful of states that recognizes ownership of property in tenancy by the entireties. Tenancy by the entireties is a unique form of ownership by husband and wife. Like joint tenancy ownership, it provides a right of survivorship. If one spouse dies, ownership of the property rests in the surviving spouse. As a result, no probate is needed for entireties property after the death of one spouse.

However, unlike joint tenancy, tenancy by the entireties provides a form of asset protection from creditors. If a creditor obtains a judgment against one spouse, the lien from such judgment does not attach to property owned by both spouses as tenants by the entireties. The creditor would have to have a judgment against both husband and wife.

To create a tenancy by the entireties, property would have to be acquired by both husband and wife at the same time. It is important that they are married at the time of the acquisition. If, for example, the two persons took title to property jointly and then were married a week later, the property would not be entireties property.

If the couple takes title as tenants by the entireties and later is divorced, the property loses its entireties character and the two own it as tenants in common. This means there is no right of survivorship and, if one dies, his or her share in the property would be subject to probate. Further, if one of the owners is subject to a judgment, the lien of that judgment attaches to his or her interest in the property.

If a married couple has a joint revocable trust, it is possible to transfer entireties property into the trust and still retain the advantages of tenancy by the entireties. The trust must have a provision that allows for property within the trust to be owned as entireties property.

The Elective Share

When the Elective Share Law was enacted in 1975, it provided that a surviving spouse was entitled to a minimum of a 30% share of the deceased spouse's probate estate. Under the law, the surviving spouse had the option of accepting what was provided under the decedent's will, or electing to take a 30% share of the decedent's net probate assets. The Elective Share did not apply to assets passing outside of probate. Since a large number of people set up trusts, transfer on death arrangements, and other vehicles to avoid probate, some estates had no probate assets. As a result, many surviving spouses were either inadvertently or intentionally disinherited.

In response to this problem, the Florida legislature passed a new bill which was signed into law on June 11, 1999, by Governor Jeb Bush, that completely revamped the Elective Share law. The new law closes the loophole by including in the Elective Share assets that do not pass through probate as well as the decedent's probate estate. The new, larger estate subject to the elective share is referred to as the "augmented estate" or "Elective Estate." Property included in the Elective Estate includes the value of:

- the decedent's probate estate
- bank accounts and investment accounts titled jointly with a right of survivorship, as well as

transfer on death accounts and other similar arrangements.

- The decedent's interest in property held as joint tenants or tenants by the entireties.
- Assets held in revocable trusts established by the decedent
- Transfers of property by the decedent in which the decedent retained a right to income or principal.
- Cash surrender value of life insurance policies on the decedent's life (not the value of the death benefits).
- Pensions and Individual Retirement Accounts.
- Gifts and certain transfers of property out of the decedent's estate within one year prior to death.
- Transfers of property made to satisfy the Elective Share.

The surviving spouse is entitled to elect to take an "elective share" which is 30% of the value of the Elective Estate. Once this amount is calculated, the statute sets forth the procedure to satisfy the Elective Share or the law will direct how it is paid. Either way the surviving spouse will receive the 30% share.

In second marriages or other situations where an Elective Share election is not desirable, it is possible for the spouses to waive their right to make an Elective Share election by a pre or post-marital agreement.

Planning For Second Marriages in Florida

In Florida, a person cannot cut his or her spouse out of an inheritance. Florida law has provisions that gave a surviving spouse a portion of the deceased spouse's estate so that the survivor is not disinherited and left destitute. This is called the "Elective Share Law."

Second marriages in Florida create a number of issues that, if not properly addressed, could make a shambles of your estate plan.

It is very common for a widow or widower to remarry. Most of these persons still plan to leave their estate to their children from the first marriage. Their trusts and wills distribute all of their assets to the children, so they see no need to change their estate planning.

However, Florida law has provisions designed to protect a surviving spouse (including a second spouse) which override the terms of a person's estate planning documents. If you are in a second marriage and wish to protect your children's inheritance, you must address these laws in your estate planning documents.

Second Marriages and The Elective Share. The first potential minefield is the elective share. As we discussed in the last section, under the Florida Elective Share law, a surviving spouse is entitled to at least 30% of the deceased spouse's estate. This means 30% of all property owned individually by the deceased spouse, 30% of all property in the deceased spouse's revocable trust and 30% of the decedent's share of property owned jointly with another person.

Under the Elective Share law, the surviving spouse can elect to claim his or her right to this share. Now, you may say, "I know my husband/wife and I agreed that neither of us would take anything from the other's estate." Even if this is true, the possibility exists that your surviving spouse may not be the one making the decision. If your spouse is incapacitated at the time of your death, all of his or her decisions would be made by the person appointed in a power of attorney or by a guardian. In either case, it is likely to be a family member of your spouse.

That family member or guardian may reason that your spouse will need the elective share to pay for his or her care.

Despite what you and your spouse talked about, they have the right to exercise the taking of the elective share.

Homestead And Second Marriages. The second scenario also involves a topic we have previously discussed: your homestead property. The Florida Constitution and Statutes give a surviving spouse rights to the decedent's homestead that overrule the terms of the decedent's will or trust.

Section 732.4015 of the Florida Statutes states that homestead cannot be devised by a will or trust if the decedent is survived by a spouse or minor child. It allows one exception: the homestead may be devised to the surviving spouse, if there is no minor child.

If you try to devise the property to someone other than your spouse, section 732.401 disallows such devise and mandates that the surviving spouse shall receive a life estate in the homestead and, at his or her death, the homestead shall go to the decedent's lineal descendants. This occurs even if you wanted to leave your home to your parents, brother or some other third person.

The Solution: The Pre-Marital Agreement. Because these laws I mentioned can completely overrule a person's wishes and estate planning, the Florida legislature has provided a way around them.

That method is the pre-marital agreement. Yes, I know that many of you picture a pre-marital agreement as something Donald Trump and other rich folks have their attorneys draw up. This pre-marital agreement is different. The purpose of this document is for you and your spouse-to-be to waive your rights to the elective share, homestead and other rights created by marriage.

The pre-marital agreement is governed by Section 732.702 of the Florida Statutes. The law states that the pre-marital agreement must be in writing and be signed by both husband-to-be and wife-to-be and two witnesses. By entering into this agreement, you can now leave your estate the way you wish without interference from Florida law.

If you wish to also provide for your spouse, you may. Only now you will do it on your own terms and not as the state mandates. In this case, you would simply include a provision in your will or trust providing for your spouse.

If you had a pre-marital agreement prepared in another state before moving to Florida, it is valid if it was valid in the state where you signed it. It would, however, be a good idea to have an attorney review it to make sure it accomplishes what you want.

Finally, you may be reading this article and saying, "Great! If only I knew about this before I got married." Don't despair. The same law provides for a post-marital agreement. This document works the same as the pre-marital, but requires both spouses to make a fair disclosure, in writing, to the other of the nature and value of their estate.

Passing On Intangible Assets:

Leaving a Legacy

It is a common belief that there is more to leave behind than the assets that you have acquired during your life. What can be even more valuable to your family are your values, ideals, hopes, dreams and lessons learned. And making a positive impact on lives in your community is a legacy that will endure for generations.

Leaving A Legacy To Your Family. Many of us have, at times in our lives, struggled to achieve success and find meaning to our existence. For some of us, that struggle continued for years while we learned through trial and error lessons that shaped our outlook and made us the persons that we are today.

Was your life experience a journey that led you to this point in time? Or did you one day have an epiphany that changed everything? Regardless of the manner in which you got here, the story of your life holds lessons and values for your loved ones.

As an estate planning attorney, I have had the experience of listening to clients as they strive to create a plan to distribute their worldly possessions after they are gone. Invariably, this conversation turns to their children. How they were when they were young. What kind of persons they have turned out to be.

Many times, these thoughts guide my clients in deciding what each child will receive. Instead of sending a message through the distribution of assets, wouldn't it be fitting if they could put their feelings in a different type of will?

That different type of will has been referred to as an "ethical will" or as we will call it, a Legacy Statement.

The ethical will is an ancient tradition which many trace back to the Biblical story of Jacob, who before his death conferred a personal blessing on each of his twelve children. The practice reached its peak in the Middle Ages and has undergone a resurgence lately.

A Legacy Statement is a publication of a message you wish to give to those you leave behind. It can take the form of many different media. While most Legacy Statements are in writing, an ever-increasing number are being delivered by audio or video recordings.

It is important to realize that a Legacy Statement is not a legal document. It may express your wishes and desires, but it should not be intended as a legally binding instrument.

A Legacy Statement allows you to deliver a personal story based on a theme you select. Legacy Statements may be long journals or brief letters. Each is as unique as its author, but most have certain elements in common.

1. *A Target Audience.* This is the object of your message and lesson. The person or persons to whom you are directing the Legacy Statement. It may be your spouse, your children, your friends, your community or anyone you intend to be impacted by your statement.

2. *A Message.* The message is the expression of the purpose for writing the Legacy Statement. You will need to decide the purpose of your Legacy Statement. Some examples of the reasons people write Legacy Statements are:

• To impart advice to those who follow you.

• To serve as a love letter to those who mean so much to you.

• To introduce yourself to future generations who will never have the honor of meeting you in person.

• To emphasize what has been important to you and has been a profound influence in your life.

• To tell your personal story; your hopes, your dreams, your disappointments. It may be a narrative of past successes and failures, an accounting of your life. Some writers use the occasion to speculate how they would do things differently if they had the chance to "do it all over again."

3. *A Lesson.* Out of the message comes a directive or lesson that you may wish to impart. You can use your life experiences to create a background for your statement of the moral and ethical principles you implore your heirs to follow.

Leaving A Legacy To Your Community. Many people feel compelled to give back to their community. After all, what better way is there to leave your legacy than by helping others? A plan of charitable giving is the action behind the words of the Legacy Statement.

There are causes near and dear to each of our hearts that we have a desire to support. Unfortunately, many people don't know how to set up a charitable plan. Even more unfortunate, many don't believe they have the resources to contribute to charity.

There are many different ways to set up a charitable program. No matter what the size of your estate, you can create a vehicle that will allow you to give to the cause of your choice, on your terms, for generations to come. Even smaller estates can create a charitable legacy that will positively impact lives. Did you know that you can reduce and eliminate estate taxes through charitable giving? That it's possible to give a large portion of your estate to charity and still have your heirs receive a larger inheritance than if you had not given?

If you have a large estate, you are going to be a philanthropist whether you plan for it or not. If you make no charitable plan of your own, your default charity will be the United States Treasury.

Estate taxes are levied at the federal and state levels and confiscate a significant percentage of all estates that exceed the maximum estate tax credit. Some high net worth individuals have engaged in estate planning to be able to pass the maximum amount allowed by law to their heirs. But in a lot of cases, part of the estate is still subject to estate taxes. For these taxpayers, their legacy is contributing to the programs and operations of the government.

Think about it. Do you believe the government is doing a good job of applying our tax money? Or do you think you can make better decisions on how that money is used?

What a lot of people don't know is that their charity doesn't have to be the government. You can control that part of your estate that is earmarked to go to the government in the form of estate taxes. How much of an impact do you think your estate tax contribution will make to society? And what will it support? Will it be a program or cause that you feel strongly about, or will it be used in a way that does not represent your values? Remember, sharing your legacy is about passing on your values.

Fortunately, the government has provided us with certain credits and deductions to apply against our estate tax liability. The most powerful of these is the charitable deduction. Any portion of your estate that you contribute to a qualified charity is not counted as a portion of your estate that is subject to estate taxation. In addition, charitable contributions provide deductions that will reduce your income tax liability and the charitable deduction can be used to actually increase the size of your estate.

Make An Impact –
Leave A Legacy.

Increasing Your Estate Through Charitable Giving. Our society encourages charitable giving. Even to the extent that our government provides significant tax benefits for it. In fact, many of these tax benefits are so favorable that they create valuable opportunities for you to support a cause you believe in, establish a legacy for you and your family, reduce your income and estate taxes, and provide tax-free distributions to your heirs. One of these charitable giving strategies is the Charitable Remainder Trust.

A Charitable Remainder Trust (CRT) is an irrevocable split-interest trust. Irrevocable means that once it is set up, it cannot be terminated at the discretion of the creator (Grantor). Also, property contributed to the trust is permanently removed from the Grantor's estate. If he needs to take back the property later, he will not be able to do so, although he can provide for income payments to himself for life.

Split-interest means that the property in the trust is shared between non-charitable beneficiaries and charitable beneficiaries. Usually, the CRT pays income to one or more non-charitable beneficiaries (typically, the Grantor and spouse) for their lifetimes or for a specified number of years - not to exceed 20. At the death of the last income beneficiary or after the specified number of years expires, all property remaining in the trust must be distributed to one or more charities.

A CRT is exempt from income, capital gain and estate taxes. The donor or grantor receives a charitable income tax deduction for the portion of the contribution that will eventually be distributed to the charity. This amount is determined by a complex IRS formula.

Any assets you contribute to the CRT can be sold by the CRT without any capital gains tax.

You can receive more income from the asset than you did before donating it to the CRT.

You can set up a wealth replacement trust to purchase a life insurance policy to replace the inheritance that was lost as a result of the CRT.

Even though the Charity will not receive its gift until later, because your contribution is irrevocable, you can manifest your legacy during your lifetime and receive recognition for your gift.

To many, the scenario I am about to describe is too good to be true. Let's start by listing the benefits of planning with a Charitable Remainder Trust (or CRT) by showing how it can solve problems you may encounter.

Problem: You have a piece of real estate that is producing no income for you. You would like to sell it and reinvest the proceeds to create a regular income, but the real estate has greatly appreciated since you purchased it and you don't want to be hit with massive capital gains taxes.

Problem: You want to create a legacy by funding a scholarship fund for disadvantaged students in your community, but the piece of real estate is the only asset you can use to fund the scholarship fund. You also wanted to use a part of the real estate to fund your children's inheritance.

How can you sell the real estate, use the proceeds to invest and provide yourself a stable income, use the proceeds to set up a scholarship fund after your death **and** provide for your children's inheritance? The answer is the Charitable Remainder Trust. To show you how this works, let's look at a fictional example:

In 1995, you and your spouse purchased a piece of vacant commercial real estate for $100,000. Lately, you have received offers of $1,100,000 for the property from a developer who wants to build a shopping center on it. You currently receive no income from the property. To the contrary, you have annual expenses for property taxes and liability insurance.

If you sell the property to the developer, you will have a capital gain of $1,000,000 (sales price of $1,100,000 less you $100,000 tax basis in the property). At a 15% capital gains rate, you would pay $150,000 in capital gains tax, leaving only $950,000 to reinvest. If you invest it at a 7% annual rate, you will receive $66,500 each year in income which will be taxed at your ordinary income tax rate. When you and your spouse have both passed away, whatever is left of the $950,000 after estate taxes can be divided between your children and the scholarship fund.

Now, let's insert the Charitable Remainder Trust into the equation. Instead of selling the real estate to the developer, you can create a CRT and donate the real estate to it. The CRT would then sell the real estate to the developer. Since it is a charitable entity, the CRT does not pay the capital gains tax. As a result, the entire $1,100,000 is available to invest.

With a Charitable Remainder Trust, you can specify what percentage return you want to receive (provided the return falls within limits determined by a number of factors, including your age). A higher return to you would reduce the amount ultimately donated to the scholarship fund and conversely a lower return would increase the donation.

Let's say you choose the 7% rate we used above. You will receive $77,000 in income each year, an increase of $10,500 from the example without the CRT. This amount would be paid to you and your spouse for a long as one of you survives.

It gets even better. In addition to the increased annual income, you will receive a charitable deduction toward your income for a portion of the contribution you made to the CRT. Since part of the contribution you made will come back to you and your spouse as an annual income, you will not receive a deduction for the entire $1,100,000. Your tax advisor would determine the present value of the total income you and your spouse would receive from the CRT based on your life expectancy and subtract that amount from your total contribution to arrive at your charitable deduction. This deduction can be applied against your CRT income, further increasing your after tax income.

Upon the death of the survivor of you and your spouse, all of the assets then in the CRT will be paid to your designated charity.

But that's not all. Using the tax savings created by the charitable deduction plus a portion of the increase in annual income, you can establish a wealth replacement trust for the purpose of acquiring a second-to-die life insurance policy that will provide a tax-free inheritance for your children. The increased income you receive as a result of the CRT can be used to fund the insurance premiums.

This is a win-win-win situation. You and your spouse win with these benefits:

1. No Capital Gains Tax on the Sale of the Real Estate

2. Charitable Income Tax Deduction

3. Increased Annual Income

4. Eliminate or Reduce Estate Tax

5. Make a positive impact in the lives of others and in the Community

Your children or other heirs win with the following benefits:

1. No Reduction in their Inheritance
2. No Probate
3. They Receive their Inheritance in Tax-Free Cash

The community wins because you have made a significant contribution that will make a difference in other people's lives.

The only non-winner is the IRS. And believe it or not, it endorses the Charitable Remainder Trust whole-heartedly. In fact, the Treasury Regulations instruct you in detail how to set up a CRT. Imagine that!

How Large Must Your Estate Be For A CRT? An attractive aspect of Charitable Remainder Trusts is that you don't have to have a large estate to benefit from it. While those who have estates large enough to worry about estate taxes can use the CRT to reduce or eliminate those taxes, those with smaller estates can take advantage of numerous opportunities.

Anyone can increase the income from their investments by transferring highly-appreciated, under-performing assets to a CRT to lock in an attractive return without losing a part of the investment to capital gains taxes.

Just about any type of property can be contributed to a Charitable Remainder Trust. As we discussed, highly-appreciated assets provide the most benefit, but cash, stock, real estate and personal property (such as valuable collections) are proper.

CRTs And Retirement Plans. Many people have large retirement funds such as 401(k) plans or Individual Retirement Accounts. These funds have been able to grow rapidly because the government allows you to defer payment of income tax on the earnings until later (usually age 70½).

The problems arise when the time comes to start removing the funds from the retirement plan. These problems become even worse after the death of the owner and the beneficiaries start to take funds out. For owners with large estates, the retirement plan is subject to estate tax. If all or a portion of the plan needs to be liquidated to pay estate taxes, the beneficiary is hit with the income tax that has been deferred during the owner's lifetime. Sometimes, with estate and income taxes, these assets can be taxed at rates of 60% to 70% for the highest tax bracket.

For this reason, an IRA, 401(k), or other qualified retirement plan is a great asset on which to name the CRT as beneficiary. You are not legally able to transfer the retirement plan into the CRT during your lifetime; however, you can name the CRT as the beneficiary. In that case, the income taxes due on the distributions received by the CRT are cancelled by the charitable deduction.

You can set up the CRT to leave your surviving spouse or children an income for life, with income tax payable only on the amounts actually distributed to them. You then can name a charitable organization or organizations of your choice to receive the property remaining in the CRT at your spouse's (or children's) death, which otherwise would, in large part, go to the IRS in taxes.

CRATS and CRUTS. There are two different types of Charitable Remainder Trusts: the Charitable Remainder Annuity Trust, or CRAT, and the Charitable Remainder Unitrust, or CRUT. In most aspects, the two trusts are the same. This difference between the CRAT and the CRUT is the way the annual income distributions to the non-charitable beneficiaries are calculated.

A Charitable Remainder Annuity Trust pays a fixed annual income based on the value of the property initially transferred into the CRAT. Therefore, if you create a CRAT, contribute $100,000 to start it, and set up an 8% annual distribution, you would receive $8,000 each year. Regardless of whether the value of the property in the trust goes up or goes down, you will still receive $8,000 each year because that is 8% of the original contribution. Even if the property in the CRAT does not earn 8%, you will receive the same $8,000. In that case, a part of the principal would be invaded to make the distribution. On the other hand, if the CRAT property earned more than 8%, you would still only receive the $8,000 annual payment.

A Charitable Remainder Unitrust pays a fixed percentage based on the value of the property in trust. However, with a CRUT, the property is valued each and every year to determine the amount distributed.

For example, if you set up the CRUT with an initial contribution of $100,000 and select an 8% distribution rate, you will receive $8,000 in distributions during the first year. At the end of the first year (and each year after), the property is revalued. If the investments in the CRUT increased in value to $110,000, you would receive $8,800 during the next year. If, however, the value of the assets decreased to $90,000, you would only receive $7,200 during the next year. This process would be repeated each year.

Because the property value is redetermined each year, you can add property to a CRUT and such added property will be taken into account in determining the distribution.

You cannot add property to a CRAT after the initial contribution.

Setting Up Your Charitable Remainder Trust. Your Charitable Remainder Trust should be set up with the help of an attorney experienced in these matters.

You should take great care in selecting the terms of the CRT since it will be irrevocable and your ability to amend the CRT will be severely limited. The persons you choose to be your income beneficiaries cannot be changed once you have signed the trust. Likewise, the annual percentage of the payments cannot be changed.

Your selection of trustee is also important. It is not a good idea for you to name yourself as trustee. If you designate yourself as trustee and as the income beneficiary, the trust property in the CRT will be included in your estate for estate tax purposes.

The trustee is responsible for investing the assets in the CRT, making the income distributions and filing the Split Interest Tax Returns with the IRS each year. The trustee must also make the distribution to the charitable organizations at the termination of the trust. Choose someone competent and trustworthy. If you are naming your Donor

Advised Fund as a beneficiary, the Community Foundation may be able to provide or arrange for trustee services.

Wealth Replacement. Now I will describe a scenario where you can use a CRT to:

1. sell a highly appreciated asset without capital gains

2. receive a guaranteed income for life.

3. receive a charitable income tax deduction.

4. eliminate or reduce your estate tax.

5. create a legacy by leaving a gift to charity at your death.

6. leave an inheritance to your heirs tax free and in cash.

This can all be accomplished by replacing the assets you have set up to leave to charity instead of your children. To do this, you would create a Wealth Replacement Trust to replace some or all of the assets you redirected to charity.

What Is A Wealth Replacement Trust? A Wealth Replacement Trust is an irrevocable life insurance trust that you create to own a life insurance policy insuring your life. If you are married, it can own a second-to-die policy insuring the lives of both you and your spouse.

Since the CRT usually produces increased income to you and provides savings in income taxes from the charitable deduction you receive from the contribution to the CRT, you can use this as a source to pay all or part of the premiums.

Upon your death (or the death of the last of you and your spouse), the proceeds of the life insurance policy will be paid to the Wealth Replacement Trust. Because the Wealth Replacement Trust is set up as an irrevocable trust, it is not included in your estate for estate tax purposes. It can distribute the entire proceeds to your children - tax free.

A Wealth Replacement Trust is an advanced planning technique with estate tax, gift tax and state law issues. You should seek the services of an experienced attorney to help you structure and implement this plan.

Getting Started

Planning is a part of life. We are constantly planning our days, our businesses, our vacations and our schedules. Planning our estate is just another side of the same topic. But because it represents a certain finality, many of us are reluctant to do it. When we plan our estate, we recognize our mortality and that makes it tough to get started. Some people even have a fear that once they begin to plan their estate, it will lead to their death. Unfortunately, the truth is, no matter what we do we get closer to the end each day.

As an attorney who has helped my clients with their estate planning for over 25 years, I have found that the clients who are the most motivated to plan their estates are those that have had to administer the estate of a loved one or friend who has died. If the loved one or friend failed to take the time to plan his or her estate, the probate process became painfully difficult, and my client was even more motivated.

Some of the circumstances I have seen that resulted from poor or no planning are:

- Children failing to receive an inheritance.
- Loved ones losing large portions of their inheritance because of unnecessary probate costs and estate taxes.
- Family businesses having to shut down or be sold.
- Life Insurance benefits having to go through probate because the beneficiaries were not updated.
- Valuable stock certificates or other assets were forgotten and never passed on to heirs.
- Probate proceedings that have lasted two, three or more years when they could have been avoided altogether.

These are just a few samples of the results of poor or no planning.

That's what the Legacy Protection Record Keeper is all about: Giving you a step-by-step procedure to get started in the estate planning process. With the information you will gather and document in the Planner, you and/or your estate planning professional will be able to assess your situation and create a blueprint to pass your estate in the most efficient, least costly (and least taxed) manner that will render the least pain upon those you leave behind to administer it.

Your wishes can be carried out, in a large part because you have made them known and have put them in writing. It all begins with organizing and planning. START TODAY – VISIT:

www.EstatePlanningInFlorida.com

AND REGISTER FOR YOUR **FREE** LEGACY PROTECTION RECORD KEEPER by filling in the form at the upper left of the webpage <u>OR</u> call my office at (941) 473-2828.

Law Offices of Dean Hanewinckel, P.A.
2650 South McCall Road
Englewood, Florida 34224
(941) 473-2828

110

Estate Planning Glossary

Advance Directive. A witnessed written document in which an individual gives instructions regarding his health care. Two common types of Advance Directives are the **Designation of Health Care Surrogate** and the **Living Will**.

Beneficiary. A person entitled to the benefits of an asset. A beneficiary of a trust is a person entitled to receive the income from trust property and/or the distribution of the trust property itself.

Creditor claim. A claim against the decedent's estate by a creditor of the decedent for a debt incurred during the lifetime of the decedent.

Death certificate. Written evidence of a person's

death issued by a government authority in the jurisdiction in which the death occurred.

Designation of Health Care Surrogate. A written document designating another person (called a surrogate) to make health care decisions on behalf of the patient.

Disclaimer. An irrevocable waiver of a right to accept an interest in property. If a person exercises his or her right to a disclaimer, the property will be distributed in the same manner as if the person exercising the disclaimer died before his or her right to receive the property occurred.

Durable Power of Attorney. A written instrument by which an individual (the principal) appoints another person (the attorney-in-fact) to act on his behalf to make decisions and act in the place of the principal regarding business, personal, property and financial matters. Unless revoked by the principal, it is valid until the principal's death or adjudication of incompetency by the court.

Enhanced Life Estate Deed. A deed creating an arrangement in which one person (the life tenant) owns a property for her life, and upon her death it passes to other persons named in the deed (remainder beneficiaries). The life tenant has the right to sell or mortgage the property and keep all of the proceeds without the consent of the remainder beneficiaries.

Estate tax. A tax levied by the federal government and some states against property owned or controlled by a decedent at the time of his or her death.

Fiduciary. A person who holds property for the benefit of another. A fiduciary is held to a high standard of care in the management and disposition of the property. Examples of fiduciaries are trustees of a trust, executors/personal representatives, or attorneys in fact under a power of attorney.

Form 706. A tax return form created by the Internal Revenue Service which is filed when a person's estate is subject to federal estate tax.

Form 1041. A tax return form created by the Internal Revenue Service to report income tax of an estate or trust.

Form SS –4. A form created by the IRS used to obtain a tax identification number.

Individual retirement account (IRA). A non-qualified retirement plan in which income tax on the income generated by the assets held in the account are deferred to a later date. The earnings in an IRA are not taxed until the owner withdraws the funds.

Inheritance tax. A tax levied by some states against the beneficiary or recipient of property received as a result of the death of another, for example, a devise in a probate estate or a distribution from the trust.

Irrevocable trust. A trust that cannot be amended. Irrevocable trusts are usually used to remove assets from a grantor's estate for the purpose of reducing or eliminating estate taxes or asset protection.

Joint tenancy with right of survivorship. A type of ownership in which two or more persons own an equal undivided interest in property. The main feature of this type of ownership is the quality that when one owner dies all legal and beneficial title to the property is vested in the surviving owner or owners.

Life estate. A type of ownership where the owner of the property only has an ownership interest until his

114

or her death. Upon the death of the owner, title to the property automatically passes to another designated person called a remainderman. An owner of a life estate cannot direct distribution of the property through his or her will.

Payable on death account (POD). A designation placed on a bank or investment account to direct that the funds in the account are to be paid to a specific person or entity at the owner's death.

Personal representative. Also known as executor. A person or entity appointed by the court to administer a probate estate.

Per stirpes. A designation of distribution in which the share of a person who has predeceased the event giving rise to that person's distribution right will be distributed equally among the next generation of his or her lineal descendents. If a member of the next generation has also predeceased the event, that members share will be distributed equally among the next generation of his or her lineal descendents.

Pour-Over-Will. A will, commonly used with a revocable trust, through which any property not titled in the name of the trust at the time of the decedent's death is "poured over" into the trust. Any assets passing through the pour over will must go through probate. The intention is that the pour over will not be used and only serve the purpose of a safety net.

Probate. The court-supervised administration of a person's estate. A person's estate may be probated pursuant to his or her will (a testate estate) or, if there is no will, pursuant to the distribution laws of the state (and intestate estate).

Revocable trust. An arrangement, usually created by a written document, in which one party (the trustee) holds and manages property of another party (the grantor) for the benefit of a third party (the beneficiary). A revocable trust is usually created to avoid probate of the grantor's estate.

Successor trustee. A person who acquires and accepts the powers and duties of a trustee if the original trustee is unable or unwilling to serve as trustee.

Tax identification number. A number issued by the Internal Revenue Service to an individual or entity under which income and expenses are reported.

Tenancy by the entireties. A type of joint ownership between husband and wife available in a limited number of states. Tenancy by the entireties affords the owners with asset protection qualities and also contains a right of survivorship.

Tenancy in common. A type of ownership in which two or more persons or entities owned an undivided interest in property. Unlike joint tenancy, tenants in common do not have to own equal shares of the property, and upon one owner's death, his or her ownership interest will be distributed pursuant to his will or intestate probate proceedings.

Transfer on death account (TOD). A designation placed on a brokerage account for the same purpose as a POD.

Trustee. A person or entity who manages or administers the property of the trust for the benefit of a third party.

Will. A written document in which a person states his or her intention to distribute his or her real and personal property at death.

About The Author

Dean Hanewinckel has been helping his clients plan their estates for almost 30 years. His Southwest Florida office is well-known for its innovative and personalized service.

Dean is the author of three published books if you include this one. ***The Official Snowbird's Guide To Becoming A Florida Resident*** is the number one authority for Florida residency. ***Manifest Your Legacy*** guides readers to making a positive impact and leaving a legacy through legacy statements and charitable giving. Both are available at Amazon.

Dean is a graduate of the University of Florida both for business administration and law, and counts his Saturdays at the Swamp as some of his most cherished days.

His wife, Nancy, and four children provide the inspiration and support for this book.